CW01476833

To Tom, Rufus and Robin.

First published in 2015
MadeGlobal Publishing
Text © 2015 Amy Licence
Images © 2015 MadeGlobal Publishing

ISBN: 978-84-944574-7-0

Richard III lived in England in *medieval* times. He was born in 1452 at *Fotheringhay Castle*. A river flowed past its thick walls and it was surrounded by fields and woods.

Richard had six older brothers and sisters. When he was a baby he was cared for by nurses and had his own special room inside the castle. As he grew up, he had *tutors* to teach him how to read and write. He would also have learned how to ride a horse. This was an important skill. There were no cars, trains or planes, so horseback was the only way to get around. He would have gone riding and hunting in the countryside around Fotheringhay. This was good training for when he grew up to be a knight.

His father was a *duke*, the most powerful man in the country, after the King himself. He was often very busy, travelling round the country. Lots of people relied on him to look after them.

All about
RICHARD III

Amy Licence

Life in a medieval castle like Fotheringhay was rather like living in a small village. Everything the family needed was to be found there: bakers, butchers, people to brew ale, fish ponds, laundries, stables, blacksmiths, a church and much more. Only wealthy families lived in the main rooms but lots of other people lived and worked there as servants. Everything was surrounded by thick walls and a moat, because enemies would often attack and try to break inside.

While Richard was a child, war broke out in England between two families, or houses. The country was ruled by King Henry the Sixth who came from a family named Lancaster. Richard's father was the leader of the family of York. Both families were the *descendants* of Edward III and both had a good claim to the throne.

Henry became ill and Richard's father helped to run the country. Henry was a gentle man and preferred to live a religious life than to go to war. Many people thought he was a good man but not a very good King. The country needed a strong leader. They wondered if someone else might do a better job.

When Henry got well again, the York and Lancaster families fought each other in battle. The Lancastrians wanted Henry VI to stay as king and for his young son to be king after him. The Yorkists wanted to have a say in how the country was run. They felt that Henry's wife, Queen Margaret of Anjou, did not like them and was not listening to them. Men put on shining armour and carried sharp weapons. Some rode on horseback and others fired arrows. This was the beginning of a long war that would last all through Richard's life. Today we call it the *Wars of the Roses*.

The King was responsible for looking after his country and he could only do this if he was well. If the King fell sick, people started to worry that he wouldn't be able to look after his country properly and it might become weak. Because of this, Kings often had several doctors in their household, to give them the best medicines and watch over their health. It was quite usual for the King's illness to be kept a secret, in the hope that he would soon get better without people noticing.

When Richard was eight, the family of Lancaster won a big battle. His father was killed. Richard's mother was worried that her children would not be safe in England. She sent Richard and his big brother George across the sea to stay with friends, where they would be away from the fighting.

Richard and George travelled on board a wooden ship to a place called the *Netherlands*. It was stormy and they were at sea for many days. At night, they slept in *bunks* in a little room called a *cabin*. They had to be very brave. At last, they got there safely. They had to stay away for a few months, until the wars were over and it was safe for them to return to England.

Then a letter arrived, bringing good news. The family of York had won another battle. The old King, Henry the Sixth had been taken prisoner. Richard's oldest brother Edward was going to be King of England instead and the boys could come home. They were very happy.

Medieval ships were made of wood and relied upon the wind to fill their large sails to make them go. This often meant a lot of waiting around as they could not set sail in still weather or sail safely in a storm. They were small and strong, but travelling in them could be rather a bumpy ride if the seas were choppy. Inside, the conditions were quite cramped, as there might be passengers, cargo, supplies and lots of men needed to help sail the boat safely. Boats were often wrecked or sunk, even in shallow waters.

Richard's mother was pleased to see him and George back safely. They went to London to see Edward being crowned as King in *Westminster Abbey* as King Edward the Fourth. There was a huge feast and everyone wore their best clothes. A golden crown was put on Edward's head. Richard was made into a *duke*. From then on, he was known as Richard, *duke* of *Gloucester*. George became the *duke* of Clarence.

King Edward lived in *Westminster Palace*. All the most important people in England went there. The palace and the people in it were called the *court*. It was good to be at Edward's *court*. There was a lot to see and do. Dancers and musicians, singers and storytellers *performed* there and the kitchens prepared wonderful food and drink. Men and women wore brightly coloured clothes and jewels but only the King and his family could wear the most expensive ones. They could wear special *furs*, purple clothes and *cloth of gold*.

Westminster Abbey is the most important church in London, perhaps in all England. It is very old, almost eight hundred years old, but an even older church stood on the same spot before. Westminster Abbey is the place where Kings and Queens of England have been crowned since 1308, using a special chair. It is also the place where they sometimes get married, and where they are buried. There are many tombs to be seen there, and a museum, if you visit London.

King Edward needed a wife. Usually Kings would marry a *foreign* princess but Edward fell in love with a lady called Elizabeth. They got married in secret. When Richard and his mother found out, they were surprised and cross. Some of Edward's advisors did not think that Elizabeth was a suitable wife for a king because she had already been married and had two sons. Worse still, her first husband had been a Lancastrian knight who had fought against Edward. He had been killed in battle. However, Elizabeth's mother was an important lady and had once been married to Henry VI's uncle. Edward and Elizabeth were happy together and she was crowned Queen of England. Soon, she was expecting a baby.

When Richard was thirteen, he was sent to live at Middleham Castle with the *Earl* of Warwick. Middleham Castle was in Yorkshire, in the north of England. There, he learned how to be a knight. He was taught how to fight and *joust*, as well as having his normal lessons.

At the castle, he met Anne Neville. She was the daughter of the Earl of Warwick. A few years later, she would become Richard's wife.

Richard grew up to be a powerful man like his father. He was given several important jobs and helped his brother Edward run the country.

Boys of Richard's class could become a page at the age of seven and a squire at the age of fourteen. They would be taught to ride a horse, handle a sword, shoot arrows and study the arts of war. They would read books about famous soldiers and study the laws of chivalry to understand the honourable way to behave. When they had finished their training, they would be knighted, by having a sword gently tapped on their shoulders. Lots of them went on to fight in battle.

However, there was soon trouble at Edward's court. A quarrel started between Edward and the Earl of Warwick. Warwick did not like the Queen or her family. He thought that Edward listened to them too much and that they were not high-born enough to give him good advice. They wanted Edward to be friendly with the Netherlands while Warwick wanted Edward to be friends with France. He *rebelled* against the King with the help of Richard's brother George and drove King Edward out of the country.

Edward escaped to the *Netherlands* and Richard went with him. There, they gathered soldiers and weapons and sailed home again to try and win back the throne. While they were away, Warwick had made the Lancastrian Henry VI king for a second time. They fought a big battle against Warwick and won. Then they fought against the family of Lancaster and won again. At last there was peace.

Edward became King again. He lived at his Westminster court with his wife and their children. Queen Elizabeth had had a baby boy while he was in the *Netherlands*. They called him Edward, after his father.

Sometimes, it was necessary to hide when your enemies were in power. The safest place to be was outside England, so people went into exile in France, Scotland, Ireland, the Netherlands and other countries close by. There, they would be able to live under the protection of another King or great Lord. George and Richard went to the Netherlands because their sister Margaret lived there. She would have been able to help them hide and arrange for their return when it was safe.

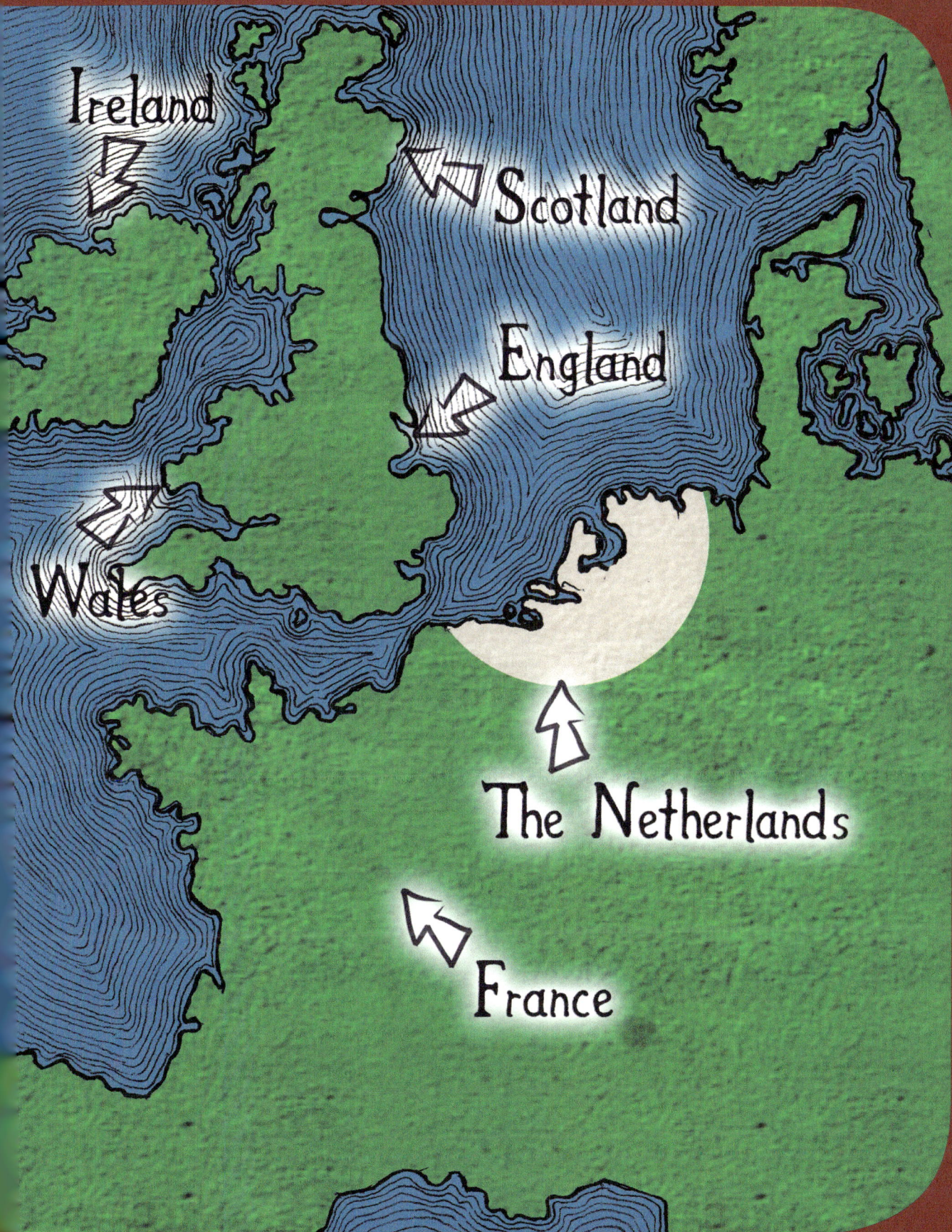

Ireland

Scotland

England

Wales

The Netherlands

France

Soon, Richard got married to Anne Neville. They made their home at Middleham Castle, where Anne had lived as a child. It was a huge, strong castle which Anne's family had made bigger and better, by building new rooms.

It was a quiet but busy life in the castle. It was a bit like a small village, with lots of buildings inside the walls. Richard and Anne had servants to cook, clean and help them dress. They had big fireplaces and *tapestries* hanging on the walls to keep it warm in winter. There were no carpets but the floors were covered with *reeds*. There was no electricity so they could not turn on lights. Instead, they used candles and lamps. They would get up early in the morning, at *dawn*, and go to bed when it got dark.

Richard was a *Catholic*. It was important to him to pray to God in church and to a number of *Saints*. There was a little church in Middleham Castle itself and a bigger one nearby. Richard and Anne would have prayed in the morning before they had breakfast and last thing at night before they went to sleep.

Richard was also a soldier. When King Edward started new wars with France and Scotland, Richard was willing to help and both the wars were won.

It could be quite cold and draughty inside castles. Kings and noblemen ordered tapestries to hang on their walls to cover the bare stone, and sometimes to cover tables. They were rather like modern carpets but they were too precious to go on the floor. Tapestries showed people from the Bible, history or mythology, like a woven painting, and a series of tapestries might tell a story. Because they were very expensive, and often made in foreign countries, they were a sign of status as only the very rich could afford them.

At Westminster, King Edward became ill and died. His oldest son was only twelve years old and should have been the next King, Edward the Fifth. Richard wanted to help him become King and went to meet him as he travelled to Westminster. Then Richard put the boy into the *Tower of London*, while he was arranging for him to be crowned.

Then Richard changed his mind. He decided that Edward should not become King after all. There were rumours that Edward's parents had not been married properly because they had been married in secret. Instead, Richard himself became King. He was crowned in *Westminster Abbey* and became known as Richard the Third.

We don't know for sure why Richard changed his mind. He may have believed the rumours about the secret marriage. Some people think it was because he did not like the Queen and did not want her to be powerful. Others think he did not want a child to be King, because as child could not give the country strong rule. Perhaps he just thought he would be a better King.

Edward the Fifth and his brother disappeared inside the Tower. No one knows what happened to them. Richard might have had something to do with it, or he might not. Even historians can't agree about it. Today we call them the *Princes in the Tower.*

In 1674, some workmen were digging in part of the Tower of London called the White Tower. They found a wooden box containing a mixture of bones. No one was sure who they belonged to, but some were small enough to have been the bones of children. Edward V and his brother Richard were aged 12 and 9 when they went missing. The bones were examined in the 1930s and might belong to the Princes. For now they are shut away in an urn in Westminster Abbey.

On the day that Richard was crowned King, there was a big *procession* through the streets of *London*. All the important people in the land followed him in their fine clothes to *Westminster Abbey*. After he was crowned, Richard was dressed in cloth of gold and sat down upon the throne. They feasted for five hours and had three thousand guests.

Richard then went on a journey all around the country. He wanted the people to see him as their new King. Not everyone was pleased though. Some people thought that Richard should not have been King at all and *rebelled* against him, including some of his old friends. The *duke* of Buckingham had helped Richard to become King but now he had changed his mind.

The family of Lancaster had not forgotten the old wars. The old King, Henry the Sixth, was dead but he had a nephew called Henry Tudor, who was living in *exile*, in France. Now Tudor and Buckingham tried to meet and remove Richard from the throne. But a bad storm stopped them and Buckingham was captured. Henry Tudor returned to France but he would be back.

When a King or Queen was going to be crowned, they went on a special journey through London. They would start at the Tower of London and dress in splendid clothes and jewels, then ride out through the streets. The city would be cleaned and decorated for them and there would be pageants or plays. Thousands of people would come out to see them ride past; sometimes the crowds pushed so much it could become dangerous. The end of the journey was Westminster Abbey, where the coronation took place.

Richard knew that Henry Tudor was planning to *invade* and take back the crown for the family of Lancaster. However, he did not know when this would happen. He carried on being King and waited for news. He tried to get the King of France to help him catch Henry but the plan did not work.

In 1485, after Richard had been King for two years, Henry sailed to England. He landed in Wales and marched towards Richard who was waiting with a bigger army. He had called all his *subjects* to help him fight but some of them did not want to because they wanted the Lancastrian Henry to become King. Henry's mother, Margaret Beaufort, and her husband, Thomas Stanley, secretly planned to help Henry instead.

The armies met near a place called Bosworth Field, in Leicestershire. Early in the morning they put on their armour and picked up their weapons. Richard had a special helmet with a gold crown on top, so everyone knew he was the King. It was against the law to fight against the King. Both sides knew that it was going to be a very important day. They said their prayers before the battle began.

England in the fifteenth century was a Catholic country. Everyone believed in the same God and most people agreed how to worship him. People then believed that God and the Saints were very close to them, watching them every day. If they needed help, or they wanted to say thank you, they could pray to a Saint or give them a gift. Most people went to church at least once a day and said prayers before breakfast and before going to sleep. Richard, Henry and their armies prayed to God to help them before the battle.

At first everything went well for Richard. He was an *experienced* soldier and fought bravely. Henry Tudor had never fought a battle before and he did not have so many men in his army. It looked as if Richard would easily win.

Then, Richard saw Henry in the distance, on his own. He thought the best way to win the battle would be to ride over to him and for them to fight each other. Richard charged! He got very close to Henry but his horse got stuck in the soft mud and he had to get down. It was difficult to fight well in the mud, particularly when he was wearing heavy armour. William Stanley had been waiting and watching the fighting. When he saw that Richard was in trouble, he brought his armies in, to help Henry win.

Richard fought bravely to the end but he was killed in battle. His crown fell off his helmet. It rolled under a bush but Thomas Stanley found it and gave it to Henry, meaning that he was now King.

Most medieval armies were made up of men who served a great lord. He would call on them to fight when he needed to, sometimes at short notice. A lot of them were already good archers, practising every day, but others were skilled in using battle axes, hammers and maces, which were a ball covered with spikes. Cannon were used during Richard's time too, but often only at the start of the battle, as they took a long time to load and sometimes went wrong and exploded. No wonder knights needed to wear armour.

After the battle, Henry took Richard into Leicester. He was carried over the back of a horse from Bosworth Field through the streets. His body was shown to all the people, who came out of their houses to see what was going on. Just days earlier, the people had seen Richard riding past as their king. He needed everyone to know that he, Henry, was now the King of England. In Leicester, there was a little church called the Grey Friars. It was a quiet and peaceful place where people prayed and sang. Henry ordered that the front part of the church floor was dug up. Here, they buried Richard the third. A little while later, Henry ordered a tomb to be built to mark where Richard lay. Richard was the last medieval King of England.

Henry became King Henry the Seventh. He was King for twenty-four years and started the Tudor *dynasty*. His son was Henry the eighth and his granddaughter was Elizabeth the first.

Many years passed. The church was pulled down and so was the tomb. The place where Richard was buried was made into a garden. Some people thought his remains had been thrown into the river. Eventually, everyone forgot that he was there. A car park was built over his grave.

Henry Tudor took the symbol of the Tudor Rose when he became King. It is sometimes called the Union Rose because it is actually a mixture of two roses, a red one and a white one. The white rose was the symbol of Richard's family, the Yorks, and the red belonged to Henry's family, the Lancasters. When Henry married Elizabeth of York, he brought the red and white families together and their symbol was painted and carved in his palaces.

But Richard himself was not forgotten. After he was dead, people still thought about him and wondered whether he had been a good man or a bad man, whether he was should have been King or not. Books were written about him and films were made.

The most famous was a play by *William Shakespeare*. Some people did not like it because in the story, Richard was a bad man with a *hunchback*. In the past, they thought that if someone had a hunched back, it showed that that person was bad. Now we know that isn't true.

Lots of people carried on thinking about Richard the third and trying to find *evidence* about his life and where he was buried.

> **"** And thus I clothe my naked villany
> With odd old ends stol'n out of holy writ,
> And seem a saint, when most I play the devil.
> - William Shakespeare, Richard III

William Shakespeare was a writer who lived a hundred years after Richard, in Stratford-upon-Avon. He is famous for writing poems and plays, including Romeo and Juliet, A Midsummer Night's Dream and Macbeth. He wrote a play about Richard which showed the way people thought about him in the late Elizabethan times. Elizabeth was a descendant of Henry Tudor, so Shakespeare's play shows Richard to be a villain, but we must remember it is a story, not a true account of history.

In 2012, a group of *archaeologists* began to dig in the car park in Leicester. They had studied old writings and maps and thought they knew where Richard had been buried, more than five hundred years ago.

All the cars had to be taken out of the car park first. Then, a digger cut through the *tarmac*. Buried underneath, they found some bones. Very carefully, they cleaned the earth around them and lifted them out of the ground. The bones were carefully placed inside a box and carried away to a safe place.

Lots of tests were carried out on the bones. The archaeologists also looked at the teeth they found in the grave and used special *methods* to find out how old they were and who they belonged to. They found out something very exciting but they couldn't tell anyone yet.

The archaeologists kept their secret and carried on doing their tests. At last, they went on television to tell everyone what they had found.

Archaeologists are people who dig through the earth to find bodies, buildings and objects from the past. They can help us understand what life was like at certain times and answer some questions, especially because not much that was written down in the past has survived. They must be very careful as they dig, scraping away layers of soil, so they don't break things buried there. The things they find can often be seen on display in museums.

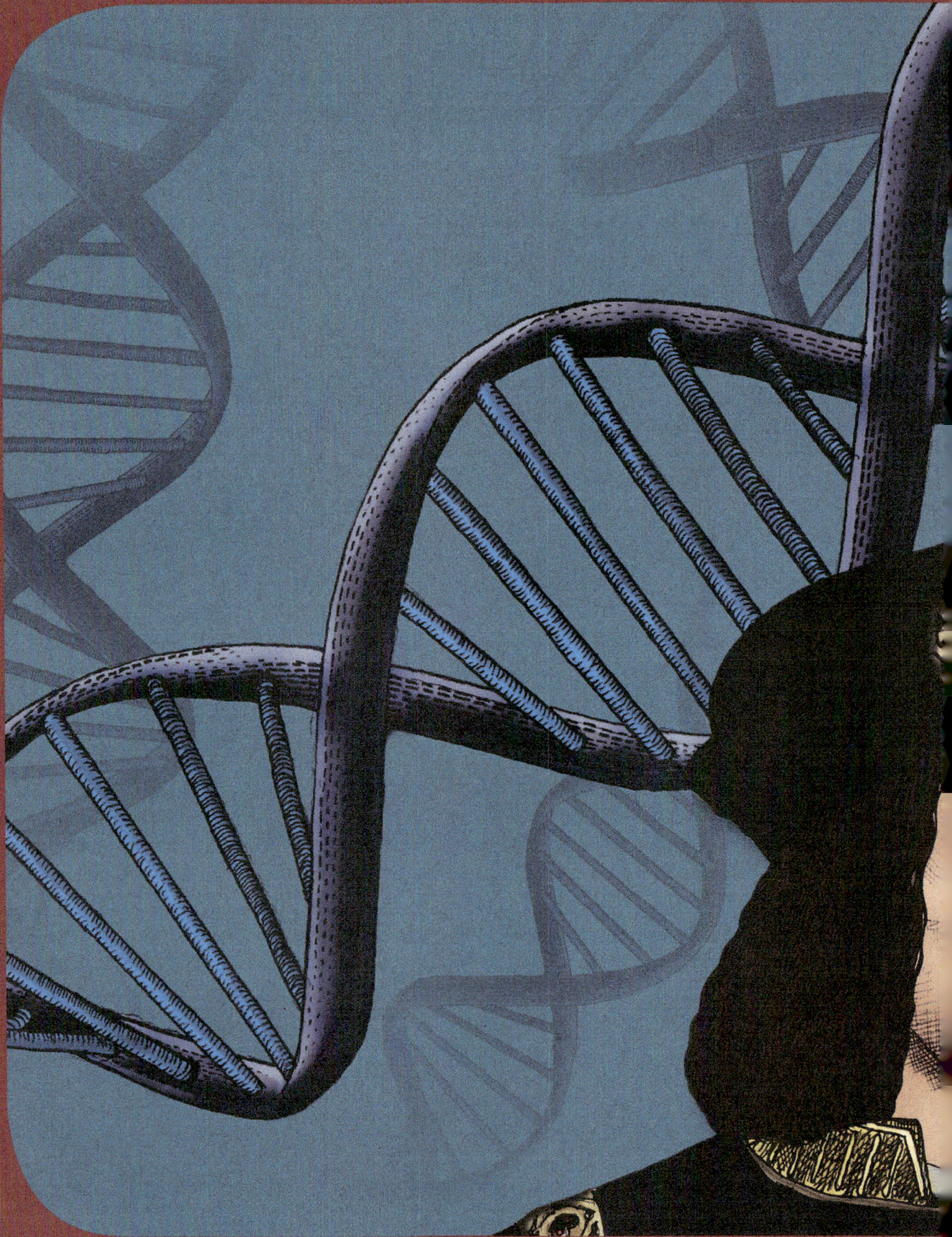

The bones had once been buried inside a church. Now the church was gone.

The bones belonged to a man.

The man had lived in medieval times.

He had been rich and could afford lots of good food to eat.

Marks on the bones showed that the man had died during a battle.

They had also tested the *DNA*. *DNA* is like a finger print inside your bones. Everyone's is different but it is passed down through families. There are people alive who are the relatives of Richard and the York family. One of them had the same DNA as the man they found.

At last it was not a secret any more.

They had found Richard the Third!

On March 26, 2015, Richard was reburied in Leicester Cathedral. Some people felt he should have been buried in York, a city he admired, or in Westminster Abbey, where his wife Anne was buried. However, a judge decided he had to be buried close to the place he was found.

Richard's coffin was carried through the streets of Leicester and many people travelled from all around the world to see him and pay their respects. Some carried white roses. The coffin was made by a man called Michael Ibsen who was descended from Richard's sister and was also a carpenter. Inside the cathedral it was decorated with a cloth called a pall, embroidered with pictures of the people who had helped to find him. A golden crown was also placed on top of it.

The reburial was shown on television. Prayers were said, songs were sung and a special poem was read. Richard's coffin was lowered into the ground and a stone tomb was placed on top. The stone contains hundreds of tiny fossils and has a deep cross carved into it. You can go and see it for yourself in Leicester Cathedral.

The church of St Martins existed in Leicester long before it became a Cathedral in 1927. A church has stood on that site for over nine hundred years, but the present one is a mixture of medieval and Victorian buildings. It has beautiful stained glass windows and thirteen bells in its tower. Now that Richard has been buried there, it has become a place of pilgrimage for visitors from all around the world. Nearby, the Richard III Visitor Centre tells the story of Richard and his discovery.

RICHARD III

Amy Licence is a historian with a special interest in the medieval and Tudor world. She became interested in history as a child, visiting castles and museums, reading books and wondering about lives people led in the past. Amy has a BA in English Literature and an MA in Medieval History and has published biographies of Richard, his wife Anne Neville, his mother Cecily Neville and his niece Elizabeth of York. She has also written about the lives of the Tudor kings and queens.

Amy is a qualified teacher and spent ten years in the classroom as well as designing syllabuses and reading lists. She has been a Leading Literacy Teacher specialising in children's literature and the use of open questions to extend learning and conducted studies into gender and genre. Amy also gives a number of talks at historical locations and on the radio and TV. She is the mother of two small boys.

Discussion Questions

1. What was Richard's childhood like?
2. What were the Wars of the Roses?
3. Why was it important that the king was healthy and strong?
4. Why do some people think that Richard should not have become king?
5. Who were the Princes in the Tower?
6. What happened to the Princes in the Tower?
7. Why did Richard lose the Battle of Bosworth?
8. Why did Henry Tudor need to show Richard's body in public?
9. How did the archaeologists know they had found Richard's body?
10. Why were people so excited when Richard's bones were found in 2012?
11. How did William Shakespeare change how people thought about Richard after his death?
12. How did they make Richard's reburial in Leicester Cathedral special?
13. What questions would you like to ask Richard if you could?
14. Why do you think people are still interested in Richard today?

All About RICHARD III

Amy Licence

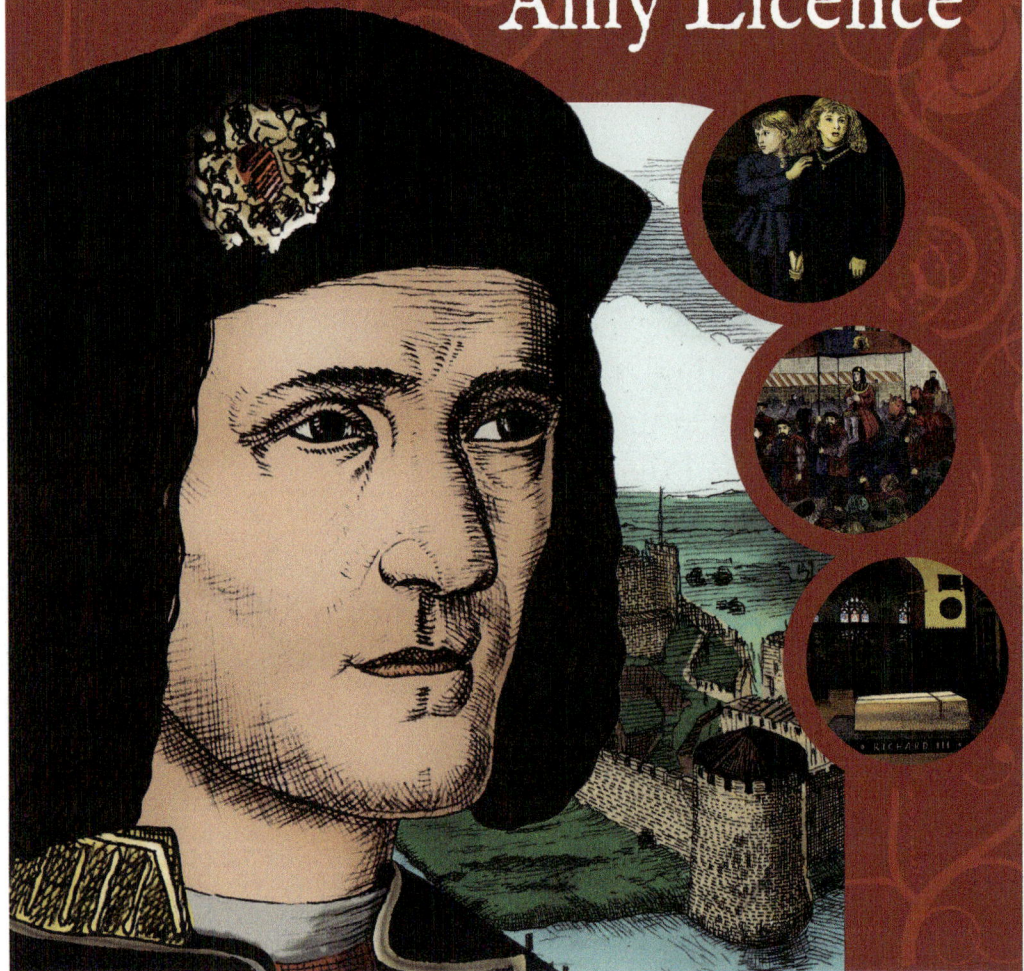

Henry VII was the first king of the Tudor dynasty. He spent a lot of his life in exile abroad and no one thought he was important. Then he raised an army and won the Battle of Bosworth and reigned for twenty-four years. He saved money, built some splendid palaces and made the country peaceful after years of war. However, he was not always safe, as plots were made by his enemies to remove him from the throne. How did Henry manage to stay king? Why was his reign so important? Read the facts about Henry VII in this book and make up your own mind.

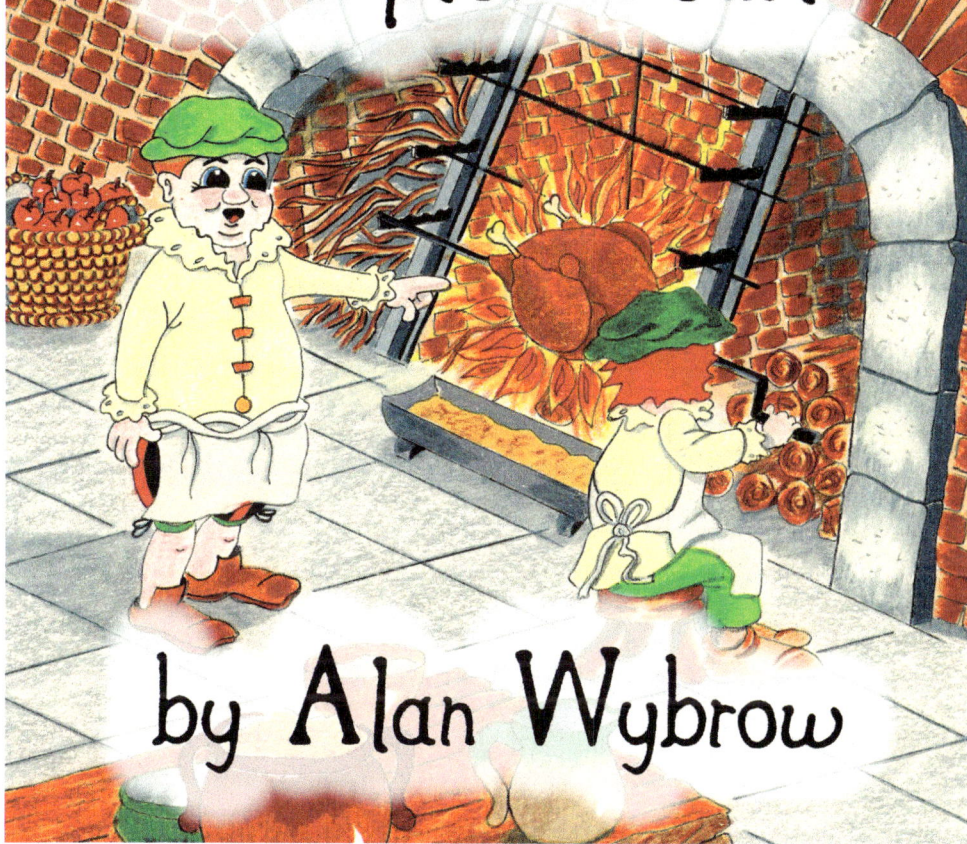

Tudor Tales
William at Hampton Court

Key Stage 1 | Ages
K - 1st Grade | 5+

by Alan Wybrow

William is a street orphan living near Hampton Court Palace. He's poor but has big dreams. Every day is the same for William, until his luck changes.
Will a life working for the king be better for William?
What adventures will he encounter?

MadeGlobal Publishing

Non Fiction History

Jasper Tudor - **Debra Bayani**
Tudor Places of Great Britain - **Claire Ridgway**
Illustrated Kings and Queens of England - **Claire Ridgway**
A History of the English Monarchy - **Gareth Russell**
The Fall of Anne Boleyn - **Claire Ridgway**
George Boleyn: Tudor Poet, Courtier & Diplomat - **Ridgway & Cherry**
The Anne Boleyn Collection - **Claire Ridgway**
The Anne Boleyn Collection II - **Claire Ridgway**
Two Gentleman Poets at the Court of Henry VIII - **Edmond Bapst**
A Mountain Road - **Douglas Weddell Thompson**

"History in a Nutshell Series"

Sweating Sickness in a Nutshell - **Claire Ridgway**
Mary Boleyn in a Nutshell - **Sarah Bryson**
Thomas Cranmer in a Nutshell - **Beth von Staats**
Henry VIII's Health in a Nutshell - **Kyra Kramer**
Catherine Carey in a Nutshell - **Adrienne Dillard**

Historical Fiction

Between Two Kings: A Novel of Anne Boleyn - **Olivia Longueville**
Phoenix Rising - **Hunter S. Jones**
Cor Rotto - **Adrienne Dillard**
The Claimant - **Simon Anderson**
The Truth of the Line - **Melanie V. Taylor**

Children's Books

All about Richard III - **Amy Licence**
All about Henry VII - **Amy Licence**
Tudor Tales William at Hampton Court - **Alan Wybrow**

PLEASE LEAVE A REVIEW

If you enjoyed this book, *please* leave a review at the book seller where you purchased it. There is no better way to thank the author and it really does make a huge difference! *Thank you in advance.*

Lightning Source UK Ltd.
Milton Keynes UK
UKOW07f1333251016
286111UK00001B/4/P